CountryLiving

Porches & Outdoor Spaces

HEARST BOOKS
New York

An Imprint of Sterling Publishing
1166 Avenue of the Americas
New York, NY 10036

ISBN 978-1-61837-156-0

Distributed in Canada by Sterling Publishing
c/o Canadian Manda Group, 664 Annette Street
Toronto, Ontario, Canada M6S 2C8
Distributed in Australia by Capricorn Link (Australia) Pty. Ltd.
P.O. Box 704, Windsor, NSW 2756, Australia

For information about custom editions, special sales, and premium and corporate purchases,
please contact Sterling Special Sales at 800-805-5489 or specialsales@sterlingpublishing.com.

Manufactured in China

2 4 6 8 10 9 7 5 3 1

www.sterlingpublishing.com

CountryLiving

Porches & Outdoor Spaces

HEARST BOOKS

New York

CONTENTS

| 1 |
PERFECT
PORCHES

IF YOUR HOME INCLUDES a classic porch, count yourself blessed. Blurring the lines between outdoors and in, this is a special place that lets you enjoy fresh air and wafting breezes while being sheltered from the sun—and relaxing in a cushioned chair or even a swing! In nice weather, it's practically a second living room. The best style for decorating your porch? That depends on the look of your home and your own taste. Traditional, rustic, retro, or flea-market funky—the choice is up to you!

OPPOSITE On the porch of this antique Rhode Island home, a vintage bridge tablecloth and soft-green wrought-iron furniture give character to a serene space.

Woodsy & Rustic

FORM MEETS FUNCTION when it comes to the no-fuss, no-frills, but definitely ready-for-fun porches of lake houses and vacation cabins. Laid-back Adirondack chairs? Check. Firewood? Naturally. Canoe paddles and maybe even a float? There's no better place to store them than the porch, and head on down to the lake.

▲ THIS VERMONT LAKEFRONT HOUSE is a low-key family retreat, starting with the white-trimmed shingled porch and welcoming white chairs.

◄ THE PORCH OF THIS 600-SQUARE-FOOT IDAHO CABIN offers stunning mountain views—and a fire pit to keep tenderfeet warm.

► AT A MODERN CABIN in a Cape Cod forest abutting a 25-acre lake, shingled walls and unvarnished wood floors and posts provide the perfect setting for a bright-red Adirondack chair, geraniums, and blue enamel buckets-turned-cachepots.

Flea-Market Chic

THE QUICKEST WAY TO GIVE YOUR PORCH CHARM unlike any other is to kit it out with well-loved objects that have stood the test of time. Second-hand finds don't have to read funky. Just take a gander at the traditional, almost formal space on page 12. Vintage pieces are versatile, mixing with other styles as accents, or working together to create their own off-hand look. Whichever way you choose to go, one thing's certain: You'll have a space that's yours and yours alone.

▶ **A PAIR OF RUSTIC WOODEN GLIDERS** dating to the 1930s has pride of place on this Ojai, California, front porch.

▼ **THIS WROUGHT-IRON DAYBED—** found locally in New York's Hudson Valley— has become the family hangout. A porcelain garden stool doubles as a table, and a bright-yellow antique French garden chair and navy striped rug deliver panache.

ON THE FRONT PORCH of this cottage on Mount Desert Island, Maine, woven round trays of varying sizes make an imposing display. A basswood moose head, rustic benches, and an Ikea basket filled with firewood add to the quirky appeal.

Collect Yourself

WHERE BETTER TO MAKE A PERSONAL STATEMENT than your own front porch? One dramatic way to do that: Display a treasured collection or other prized objects. Artifacts, seashells, hats, bags, bottles—humble on their own, they have appealing impact in numbers. Sometimes, more *is* more.

▲ **BEAUTIFULLY ARRANGED** on a rustic table, prized shells and antique bottles create a lovely still life at a Granville, Ohio, home.

◄ **PRACTICALLY SPEAKING:** Sun hats and extra totes hang out on the shingled porch of this Fire Island beach house. Also on display: antlers and a sisal-covered boat bumper.

Interior Style Goes Outside

THANKS TO WEATHER-RESISTANT FURNISHINGS, fabrics, and even artwork, outdoor rooms can easily rival their interior counterparts. Dramatic drapes provide shade, privacy, and warmth on a chilly night. An eye-catching enlarged family photograph is a striking focal point. Add comfy cushioned seating, and there's really no reason ever to spend a summer afternoon inside again.

▲ **DURABLE ENAMELWARE PLATES** bring interior panache out to the porch.

➤ **WHY SHOULD INTERIOR WALLS HAVE ALL THE FUN?** Give your porch living-room polish with a favorite snapshot printed on weather-resistant vinyl.

▲ **A DRAMATIC FRAMED MIRROR REFLECTS THE YARD**—and a great sense of outdoor élan—in this Arkansas home.

➤ **THE WHITE CURTAIN** on this porch in Ohio can enclose the space for extra coziness on cool or rainy days. String lights and an antique folding card table also enhance the sense of being indoors.

A CREWELWORK FOOTSTOOL,
wall mirror, and comfortable furniture
in weather-resistant fabric elevate
this wide front porch.

IT'S CURTAINS FOR BORING OUTDOOR AREAS: These add drama and help filter the daytime sun.

AT THIS C. 1870 HUDSON RIVER VALLEY FARMHOUSE, the color scheme of the dark-green standing-seam roof and trim (see inset) extends to a striped floor on the porch. A pachysandra border surrounds the outdoor space.

Traditional Style Secrets

ALWAYS AS FRESH AND BRIGHT as a summer day, white wicker never goes out of fashion. It's versatile enough to pair with virtually any other color, but dark green is a timeless favorite, evoking images of beloved New England summer camps.

◀ CLASSIC GOOD LOOKS ON THE CHEAP: The owners of this Hamptons beach house nabbed wicker chairs for $10 each at a rummage sale and outfitted them with cushions from Kmart. For around $45 per shrub, quick-growing hydrangeas give a porch more privacy than railings—and there's no carpenter required!

▼ TIMELESS TOUCH: A straw bee skep keeps things abuzz on this Sonoma, California, porch.

THE POWER OF PAINT!

PAINT GIVES YOUR PORCH POLISH and protects it from the elements. For bare wood, use a primer. If the wood has already been painted, lightly sand the surface to improve adhesion, making sure to scrape and spot-prime peeling areas. Apply one to two coats of paint made for high-traffic zones. Or, choose a deck stain to let the wood's natural beauty show through.

Refresh and Revamp

PAINT AND FURNISHINGS are the tools of any home makeover. On a long, narrow porch (far right), white rockers blend with the light-colored exterior walls for a soothing, well-ordered look. In the outdoor living room (below), simple, functional, affordable pieces in neutral hues create a backdrop for red, white, and blue pillows that deliver punch.

BEFORE

ONCE EMPTY EXCEPT FOR A HANGING SWING, this Florida porch is now a comfy neighborhood gathering spot, thanks to a few well-chosen accessories—most ordered online. Particularly notable: weather-resistant panel curtains, bold accent pillows, sturdy woven polyurethane chairs, and a waterproof mat that defines the space and gives it a larger look.

BEFORE, THIS MICHIGAN CAPE COD—STYLE HOME was a mishmash of different woods and disparate materials. Now, a light color scheme unifies the place inside and out. A quartet of white rockers and a black hanging swing welcome guests on the front porch.

BEFORE

MAKE IT YOURS

As practical as they are pretty, these affordable ideas add up to a porch with living room appeal.

(1) Turned upside down, **a galvan-ized planter becomes the perfect perch for drinks.**

(2) **A faux-bois floor lamp** feels indoor-worthy, yet slyly references the great outdoors.

(3) **These curtains,** made of weather-resistant fabric, sport a bold print on the inside—and a stripe on the side the neighbors see.

(4) **The deeper your seating,** the more pillows you need to pile on.

(5) **The washable cover** on this day-bed's twin mattress gives it the look of professional upholstery.

(6) **A reversible recycled-plastic rug** doubles the return on your investment.

(7) **Woven wicker chairs** and an earthy wooden table keep the décor grounded.

23

| 2 |
SCREENED & ENCLOSED
PORCHES

WHETHER THEY'RE PROTECTED from the elements by screens, glass, or actual walls, enclosed porches magically give you the feeling of being outside—and all that has to offer—without any of the negatives (like bugs!). The sturdier the enclosure, the more the furnishings and décor can incorporate the characteristics of indoor furniture, such as upholstery. Still, even an enclosed porch remains a porch, and some of the most charming spaces are decorated with objects that reflect that humble identity: rustic wood, wicker, and rattan. Whimsical old signs and found objects that might be out of place in a formal room are perfectly at home in these more casual areas.

OPPOSITE The enclosed front porch of this Maine country cottage shelters an iron-and-brass daybed sporting a vintage seersucker coverlet. It's a favorite perch for the owner's petite pooches.

Call of the Wild

ROUGH-AND-READY LOOKS REMINISCENT OF THE GREAT NORTH woods are right at home in indoor-outdoor spaces. Hallmarks of the motif? Twiggy furniture, rich reds and greens, and antlers, of course!

➤ **AT THIS MICHIGAN CABIN,** the owners used sturdy chains and hooks to turn a bench into a swing. It joins a similarly rustic chair and love seat on the screened-in front porch.

▲ **A DRAMATIC AUSTRIAN ANTLER BENCH** gives the potting room and sun porch of a Rhode Island home the most civilized sort of untamed style.

Great Escapes

VACATION HOME PORCHES are particularly well suited to a not-too-polished, woodsy look. Keeping décor simple and low-key is a clear signal that it's time to put the iPhone away.

▼ **ON NEW YORK'S FIRE ISLAND,** an enclosed front porch doubles as a guest room, thanks to a built-in daybed decorated with pillows from West Elm. On the wall? Turtle shells—an antique-store find.

◄ **THE COZY ENCLOSED PORCH OF THIS 1778 VERMONT FARMHOUSE** still retains its unfinished sloping ceiling. Below, wooden furniture and earth-toned pillows round out the north-woods vibe.

THIS GLASSED-IN NEW HAMPSHIRE PORCH is flooded with sunlight year-round. White trim and sofa cushions complement the natural wood and keep the feeling airy and bright.

Clean And Natural

A FRESH ALTERNATIVE to the darker, woodsy look? Lighten things up. Pale or white tones, natural wood, and simple lines come together to create comfortable, more contemporary spaces that are still simple, unfussy, and thoroughly unpretentious.

▼ MADE FROM RECYCLED ALUMINUM FRAMES AND RECLAIMED CYPRESS, the wicker chair and sectional on this screened-in porch give a light, serene feeling with help from the cool blue tones of the cushions and pillows. The natural floor and plank-top table provide a hint of country.

Rough-Hewn and Relaxed

A PORCH DOESN'T HAVE TO BE FANCY—or large—to bring charm to the home it graces. A small screened-in riff on a mudroom, a straight-forward dining area (enlivened with string lights), and a seating area with striking chairs and dramatic plants all deliver pleasure delightfully out of proportion to their size.

▲ **SURROUNDED BY BEACH GRASS** and covered with ivy, this Rhode Island beach house boasts a tiny screened-in porch at the rear just big enough for an ornate wicker chair.

◄ **IN AN OHIO CABIN,** molded fiberglass chairs from the Brimfield Antiques Market offer welcome seating.

► **ON THE SCREENED-IN PORCH OF THIS SOUTH CAROLINA VACATION HOME,** a picnic-inspired table and benches, an elegant potted palmetto, and festive string lights create an easy space where the owners gravitate for every meal.

A WROUGHT-IRON LIGHT FIXTURE
and an ebony gateleg table transform
the screened-in back porch of this
Michigan home into a real dining room.

Refined Redefined

NOT EVERY PORCH IS RELENTLESSLY CASUAL. Serious furniture, like an ebony table (left), or inspired lighting, such as a chandelier or column lamps (below), can take a potentially relaxed area in an entirely different direction.

▼ **IN CHATTANOOGA, TENNESSEE,** a screened-in side porch goes glam with a sheltering awning, elegant wicker, and floor lamps inspired by Greek columns.

Second Time Around

ONCE AN OUTDOOR PORCH, ALWAYS AN OUTDOOR PORCH? Not at all. These spaces can live new (indoor) lives as mudrooms, entryways, halls—the options are limitless. The best choices, though, are rooms that want to be a little rough around the edges, so the area can retain the integrity of its original purpose.

➤ **THIS FUNKY MAINE COTTAGE'S** mudroom still bears the white shingled walls of its previous life as a porch. The hand-painted sign found on a North Carolina roadside strikes a tongue-in-cheek note perfectly in keeping with the home's style.

▲ **THE MAIN HALL OF THIS 1906 CALIFORNIA HACIENDA** was originally a porch. Now it sports a 19th-century barber pole, a reproduction Windsor bench, and rugs by Woodard & Greenstein.

Dramatic green shutters provide a backdrop for whimsically patterned upholstery and charming pillows in this Florida cottage.

(1) **An indoor-outdoor rug:** Lay the groundwork for a cozy, homey space with a floor covering. The indoor-outdoor variety can stand up to drinks and snacks.

(2) **Splashes of color:** Neutrals are great for background pieces, but add colorful accessories for a porch that says "fun." Striped pillows and a bright-red accent table set the right mood.

(3) **Bountiful blossoms:** Bouquets of flowers are always welcome. It really isn't possible to have too many!

(4) **A useful coffee table:** Rattan, casual wood, or metal versions are at home outdoors and give guests a place to rest a coffee mug—or they can double as a bar.

(5) **Comfy, casual seating:** Look for seats that make sense outside (the hanging swing and rattan "pretzel" chairs at left are perfect) but also offer guests a soft, cushioned place to plop down.

| 3 |
LET THE OUTSIDE IN
SUNROOMS & MORE

LIGHT-FLOODED INDOOR SPACE are the next best thing to the actual outdoors. (And on bright winter days, of course, they're even better, since they let you soak up the sunshine without enduring chilly temperatures.) Some homes have sunrooms, which exist for the express purpose of basking in the rays indoors. Others have rooms that aren't sunrooms per se, but boast plenty of windows. When the sun pours in on nice days, everyone's spirits are brightened. If you're the owner of one of these charmed spaces, don't miss the opportunity to enjoy it to the max!

OPPOSITE Bright yellow walls and a rattan sofa make sure that this indoor "winter porch" always seems summery. A rough-hewn coffee table and nature-themed throw pillows enhance the room's laid-back vibe.

Here Comes the Sun

A WINDOW-FILLED ROOM comes with a major decorating rule it's wise to observe: Don't block the light! Opt for sheer curtains (or none!) and give those wonderful windows the respect they deserve. Play up the outdoor feeling with casual furniture, rugs, and plants.

▼ **SO MANY DETAILS** bring the outdoors inside this cheery room in Upstate New York: the yellow-painted muntins of the six-over-six windows; the Pottery Barn seagrass chairs; and abundant potted ferns and flowers.

SHEER PANELS make the most of the sunshine in this rustic California cabin. Instead of a giant plasma TV, a 10-foot projection screen pulls down from the ceiling—and goes back up, preserving the sunlight and the view.

WHO WOULDN'T WANT TO WAKE UP TO THIS BRIGHT-YELLOW breakfast nook, furnished with a built-in bench, a scalloped-top pedestal table from Ethan Allen, and a darling orange chair?

Rise and Dine

A BREAKFAST ROOM *should* be the sunniest place in the house! And white or bright walls enhance the light even more. When you have spaces like these, sleeping in may lose its appeal!

▼ **OVERSIZED WHITE WINDSOR CHAIRS,** reminiscent of *Alice in Wonderland*, are perfect for this dramatic white breakfast area. French doors open to let the morning breeze waft in.

Almost Alfresco

EVERY MEAL IS A SPECIAL OCCASION when you have a dining room that blends seamlessly with the backyard or garden. On beautiful summer days, throw open the doors and catch the breeze. When the weather's not quite as cooperative, glass doors still bring a helping of greenery and sunshine to the table.

➤ **GORGEOUS FRENCH DOORS** topped with a transom capitalize handsomely on the great outdoors in the dining area of this clean country-style Georgia lake house.

▲ **WHITE MAKES RIGHT** in this upbeat breakfast nook. Bright-white banquets, sheer curtains, and a 1960s chandelier keep the mood light, while a salvaged wood table, metal stools, and high-impact turquoise cushions round things out.

ONCE AN EXTERIOR PASSAGEWAY between the main house and garage, this dining room acknowledges its outdoorsy past with glass doors that open onto the garden.

NICKEL-PLATED SCHOOLCHAIRS and other silver-toned touches reflect the abundant light in a Long Island, New York, kitchen.

The DIY Sunroom

THIS 1745 WOODBURY, CONNECTICUT, HOUSE didn't have a sunroom—so the owner built one, inspired by the home's history and surroundings. The brick floor and stone walls imply that the room was once a terrace, now enclosed. Who can object to a little decorating sleight of hand when it all comes together so beautifully?

▼ **THE NEW SUNROOM** in this 18th-century home was designed to look as if it were added in the 19th century. Windows boast views of the beautiful gardens outside, and potted plants bring nature inside.

◄ **OLD MEETS NEW** in the same sunroom's seating area. The casement windows are salvaged and the fireplace surround is vintage, but the PlexiCraft table is unmistakably of the moment.

Front-Row Seats

WHEN YOU HAVE A LIVING ROOM that looks out on a spectacular view, furnishings must be selected accordingly. That means minimal window treatments and colors that complement rather than compete with the vista.

▶ **NICE AND NAUTICAL:** A subtle blue-and-white striped theme pays homage to the watery scene outside.

▲ **A MELON-COLORED TABLE** pops against neutral chairs and a seafoam sofa. Roll-up rattan shades make way for the Cape Cod view!

Woodland Reveries

A HOUSE IN THE WOODS can easily be dark and dreary. But when there are windows like these, light pours in and the soothing green view becomes a part of the room—almost like a painting.

▼ **INDOORS, LEATHER ARMCHAIRS** pair with a nubby linen sofa. On the porch just outside, a rocking chair invites visitors to meditate on the trees just beyond.

◄ **EVEN THE BRIGHT STRIPED RUG** and colorful geometric pillows in this otherwise neutral room are right in sync with the home's natural, woodsy setting.

Dreamy Views

LIVING AREAS AREN'T THE ONLY ROOMS that can benefit from taking note of what lies just outside. Bedrooms with adjoining porches, terraces, or patios are truly special, whether you sleep there every night, or just as a (lucky) houseguest.

> **THIS BEDROOM** in a Canadian lake house faces a garden and gets lots of cheery morning light. So the owner took a bright, fresh approach, with subtle pale blues set off by a tomato-red ikat pillow.

▲ **AN ALL-WHITE BUT THOROUGHLY LOW-KEY** master bedroom in this Cape Cod–style cottage in Michigan's Harbor Country opens onto a porch. It's the perfect place to enjoy a morning cup of coffee—with a little nature on the side.

| 4 |
DECK OUT THE
PATIO
& DECK

THERE'S SOMETHING ABOUT A PATIO OR DECK that says "Come on over!" Whether you outfit it with a table and seating for casual meals, or just a couple of comfy chairs where you and a friend can settle in for a good long chat, these are spaces meant for great times. Get ready for company!

OPPOSITE On the back patio of this Martha's Vineyard home, a marble-topped table, built from old railroad ties, pairs with African chairs that repurpose oil drums. 'Annabelle' hydrangeas line the stepped path beyond.

Mix and Match

PATIO FURNITURE doesn't have to come as a set from a store. The owners of the two patios here found ways to bring creativity and originality to their outdoor spaces that reflect their locale and personal passions.

➤ ON THIS TEXAS HILL COUNTRY PATIO, metal folding chairs in varied bright shades offer a colorful contrast to a table built out of local limestone.

▲ A HOMEMADE PATIO of slate and gravel is the perfect match for an assortment of metal chairs the homeowner picked up at antiques markets and repainted "at whim." The chairs pull up to a long table that's made of two $100 Pier 1 tables, combined by the clever North Carolina homeowner and her husband.

Please Be Seated

NO MATTER THE ERA, vintage chairs bring charm, character, and a touch of class to patio dining areas. Don't worry about searching out a matching table. Modern classics pair wonderfully with many other styles—and a pretty tablecloth is always an option!

▼ **FRENCH 1940s CAFÉ CHAIRS** and a tag-sale table welcome guests to this plant-filled Alabama patio.

SHOW YOUR METAL

IRON FURNITURE INTRODUCES a refined (and in some cases retro) note to a patio. Wrought iron is prized for its sturdiness and craftsmanship, and is bent and hammered into shape by hand. Mold-made cast-iron items, on the other hand, are bolted together, and sometimes have visible seams. Blacksmiths in America popularized wrought iron during the 1920s, and it remained in vogue until the Eisenhower era, when lighter, cheaper, rustproof aluminum caught on. Vintage American-made wrought iron is now highly coveted. Look for nicely rounded wire ends and sturdy tables that don't shake, as well as substantial curved feet that won't sink into the grass. To test whether a piece is wrought iron or aluminum, use a magnet. If it sticks, you're probably looking at the real deal. Once you've brought your treasure home, protect it with a coat of marine varnish, or paint it. (Painting an antique won't diminish its value.) Although it's strong enough to sit outside year-round, wrought-iron furniture rusts easily, so inspect your furniture every year and if you see any rust, sand it away and cover the spot with primer and paint.

Rustic Simplicity

AN EASY COUNTRY LOOK is perfect for patio style. Go super clean-cut with a straight-ahead picnic table, barn doors, and a gaily striped awning. Or think South—as in South of France—with wicker, a pine table, and a gravel patio surface. Who wouldn't want to spend Sunday—or every day—in the country?

▼ **FRAMED BY A CHEERY YELLOW-STRIPED AWNING** made of Sunbrella fabric, this patio has sliding barn doors that open to allow the outdoors to merge with the indoor kitchen (and let the cook be part of the party!).

◄ **WICKER CHAIRS FROM TARGET SURROUND AN ANTIQUE PINE TABLE** on a gravel patio in Glen Ellen, California. Olive trees border either side.

California Dreamin'

THERE'S NOTHING ELSE LIKE THE STYLE that's come together in the Golden State. Spanish colonial and Old West influences right out of the history books meet rustic meet Provençal (a perfect match, thanks to the climate) meet luxe. It all adds up to easy comfort, perfect for enjoying the outdoors year-round.

▼ **THIS LOS ANGELES HOME** pairs mismatched woven chairs and a teak table on a gorgeous loose stone patio for a Provence-meets-SoCal look.

MILD SOUTHERN CALIFORNIA WEATHER AND A FIREPLACE work together to make this outdoor living area a year-round hangout. Wicker chairs from a local shop circle a coffee table fashioned from a reclaimed wine barrel.

MIDWAY BETWEEN THE MAIN RED BARN AND THE HOUSE on a Vermont flower farm, this stone patio brims with lobelia, daylilies, nasturtium, and garlic chives. The Adirondack chairs are from classic New England purveyor L.L. Bean.

Sit a Spell

WHEN IT'S TIME TO CHILL, a patio with seating is just the place. It doesn't have to be elaborate—Adirondack chairs (left) are the very soul of simplicity. And if you don't have a patio, consider creating one with gravel or flagstone—either right outside a door or in a pretty spot on the property.

▼ **VINTAGE WROUGHT-IRON SEATING** and cushions covered in outdoor gingham fabric sit happily on a leafy gravel patio in a Rhode Island retreat.

Rock-Solid Luxe

THE OWNERS OF THIS HOME START EACH DAY WITH COFFEE in front of the towering stone fireplace and may end it with a relaxing soak, gazing at the smaller patio beside the tub (opposite). In warm climates like Southern Arizona, indoor-outdoor living makes beautiful sense year-round.

▼ **WALLS BUILT FROM LOCAL COBBLESTONE** surround this rustic-luxe patio (with fireplace!) in Scottsdale, Arizona.

▶ **IN THE SAME SCOTTSDALE HOME, THE MASTER BATH** opens onto another patio, complete with an outdoor shower.

Bring On the Fun

ADDING ON A DECK—or making the most of the one you have—is a great way to squeeze extra pleasure from your home. As renovations go, the addition below is relatively minor. But if that's too big a project, consider the chalked "chess board" on the opposite page. Ten minutes max and you're ready to enjoy.

BEFORE

▲ ORIGINALLY, THE REAR OF THIS 1850s AUSTIN, TEXAS, HOME had little to offer besides a rickety gazebo (see above). But after the owners added more windows, a deck, and steps leading down to the regraded and resodded lawn (and tore down the gazebo), the backyard became a favorite gathering place.

➤ AT A FIRE ISLAND, NEW YORK, BEACH ESCAPE, Chinese wisteria and a hydrangea shrub give the cedar deck a sense of enclosure. Once inside, guests can play chess, thanks to a few chalked lines and oversize game pieces.

Hit the Deck(s)

PERCHED ABOVE GEORGIA'S LAKE BURTON, this boathouse with double-decker decks is clearly party central. The takeaway? A roof deck could add extra room for fun on top of any sturdy outbuilding!

➤ **THE OWNERS ADDED STAIRS AND A ROOFTOP DECK** to an existing boathouse, creating even more outdoor entertaining space. The tin star hails from a flea market.

▲ **THE DÉCOR ON THE ROOF DECK** of this Georgia boathouse strikes a patriotic note in red, white, and blue. Adirondack chairs and midcentury bentwood seating are joined by a coffee table crafted by a local artisan.

MAKE IT YOURS

The ultimate space for summer entertaining? An open-air dining room equipped with all the comforts of home.

① Ceiling strategy: Grommeted panels—stitched from weather-resistant fabric—attach to the home's exterior walls with hooks to form a sheltering "roof." The porous material diffuses sunshine and lets rain pass through. (With inexpensive canvas, rain will pool and could rot the cloth.)

② Dapper pennants (aka, cotton remnants cut into triangles) make a cheap no-sew banner. Use twine to tie the top two corners to a length of hemp rope, and give them a quick spritz of Scotchgard to increase their durability.

③ Mirrors on the wall help give the patio the feel of a real room—plus, they bounce the light around. A little weathering only adds to the charm.

④ Skip the plastic furniture and search out quality pieces, such as this wooden picnic set (nabbed on Craigslist for $100) and the midcentury iron seat.

⑤ A variety of wooden containers— filled with hibiscus, a prayer plant, and assorted grasses— softens the patio's perimeter, acting as a foil for the concrete floor and rocks.

⑥ A handsome recycled-plastic rug grounds the space.

| 5 |

NOOKS, RETREATS
& PRIVATE SPACES

GARDEN DESIGNERS often talk about creating "outdoor rooms" by artfully arranging plantings. But that takes time and effort. Furniture is a shortcut way to define an outdoor space, emphasizing its possibilities as a place for relaxing and enjoyment. Even a casual chair or bench says, "Stop, stay a while. Take pleasure here." If there's a gorgeous view, or a beautiful garden, all the better.

OPPOSITE The hot, bold hues of these chairs draw attention to the view beyond— and beckon a visitor to have a seat.

Simple Seating

NO NEED FOR FANCY. Standard summer chairs like slings or the butter-fly variety can be temporary or all-summer-long additions that transform virtually any area into a place to kick back alone or with a friend—and a pitcher of lemonade.

▼ **A PAIR OF STRIPED SLING CHAIRS** and a small table turn a flower border into the backdrop for the kind of leisurely summer afternoon you dream of all year long.

The addition of butterfly chairs and pillows on a lakeside dock make this spot an appealing hangout.

Bench Warming

**THE OPTIONS FOR CREATING "SECRET GARDEN" NOOKS
ARE ENDLESS.** Surrounded by a classic round bench, a majestic tree
provides seating—and a place to dream—as well as shade. A humble raised
bed in a vegetable garden offers a lush green backdrop for a bench. Dare
to go for the unexpected, and you'll end up with something special.

▲ **A SUCCULENT WREATH** adorning a
redwood fence brings a touch of style to
an unusual location.

◄ **A WEATHERED WOODEN AND
IRON BENCH** in a California garden
nestles up to a raised bed brimming with
watermelon vine, horseradish, and yellow
squash, creating an unlikely (and all the
more delightful) spot for a garden moment.

➤ **WHO COULD RESIST STOPPING
TO TAKE A SEAT** on this round tree
bench and let time go by?

TEA IN THE GARDEN: A rustic bench under a tree becomes a comfy outdoor banquette with the addition of pillows and a table. Fare suited to the *Alice in Wonderland* ambience? Pots of hot orange pekoe tea, and sandwiches made with homemade bread and early summer tomatoes.

85

Outdoor Characters

VINTAGE GARDEN FURNITURE HAS A CHARM ALL ITS OWN. Even a single chair is enough to create the kind of secluded nook that makes you want to while away the afternoon. And a collection of chairs pulled up to a primitive table says welcome to a whole gang of friends.

▼ **A $35 FLEA-MARKET SCORE** beside a galvanized trough filled with portulaca, cherry tomatoes, and other plants gives a functional container garden hangout appeal.

◄ **APPLE TREES SERVE AS THE WALLS** for this gated, gravel-floored entertainment area in Ojai, California, but the stars of the show are the 1940s café chairs paired with a distinctive table that's belonged to the homeowner for years.

Up Against the Wall

ANCHORED BY THE PRESENCE OF OUTDOOR STRUCTURES—a barn and a garden shed—these alluring dining areas offer an alternative to the usual patio just outside the back door. Lush plants—many in pots—provide a setting reminiscent of Provence.

➤ **IN UPSTATE NEW YORK,** an assortment of bistro tables and chairs is right at home next to the barn.

▲ **AN AREA WITH CONTRASTING LIGHT AND SHADE** was potentially awkward, but the homeowners successfully transformed it into a cozy dining area. *Hydrangea petiolaris* thrives in the shade provided by a north-facing potting shed wall, while desert agaves absorb the bright daytime light.

Take a Snooze

NO NEED TO RESIST THE URGE FOR A NAP when your yard boasts an inviting hammock. Hello, Sandman!

▲ **A GREEN-STRIPED HAMMOCK** suspended between two trees is the very epitome of a lazy summer afternoon.

▶ **IN THIS NEW YORK HOME,** a hammock hangs between two maple trees near the front porch. A convenient cement side table is just an arm's length away.

| 6 |
GARDEN SHEDS, PERGOLAS
& OTHER STRUCTURES

WHEN THE WEATHER'S FINE, who wants to miss a single moment of outdoor pleasure? Maximize the possibilities by creating shelters on your property. They can be humble—like the rustic pergola at left—or grand structures inspired by traditional garden conservatories. And take advantage of what already exists: With just a little ingenuity, an underutilized storage shed can become a prized location for parties and get-togethers.

OPPOSITE This rose-laden arbor in East Hampton, New York, provides the ideal spot to entertain and relax.

The Living Is Easy

WHY PERGOLAS ARE PERFECTION: Between the shelter of a vine-covered roof and the support of a stone floor exists an open-walled space that begs for comfy furnishings—and creates a backdrop for the kind of summer afternoons you remember for a lifetime.

➤ **NORTHWEST OF TORONTO, THIS RUSTIC CEDAR PERGOLA—** planted with climbing roses, golden hops vine, hardy kiwi, and grapes—offers a shady, scenic spot to enjoy the views, scents, and sounds of the garden.

▲ **BOXWOODS BACK UP A WISTERIA-COVERED** pergola in Litchfield, Connecticut.

Fly the Coop

A LITTLE CREATIVE THINKING can lead to new places for work—or, better yet, R&R. When they work in the chicken-coop-turned-studio opposite, the owners are inspired by the garden and the birds, easily viewed through the huge windows. The garden shed below retains its original function, but a front porch (with hammock) ensures that it's not all toil and no rest for this homeowner.

◄ **ONCE A CHICKEN COOP,** this structure now serves as a studio for the homeowners.

▼ **THIS BACKYARD GARDEN SHED** in Birmingham, Alabama, offers extra living space courtesy of a porch strung with a classic hammock.

Work It!

SOMETIMES A TOOLSHED IS A TOOLSHED. Sometimes a barn needs to be a barn. These functional spaces show that work areas can be beautiful as well as practical—whether they take a stylish route or simply embrace their purpose.

▼ **ON A VERMONT FLOWER FARM,** the gorgeous blossoms that are this homeowner's stock in trade contrast beautifully with the rough-hewn barn.

◄ **A PENNSYLVANIA TOOLSHED** gets a stylish update with a Carrara marble floor and iron lanterns that formerly hung in a Kentucky church. A lush fern in a silver-footed urn adds a note of unexpected elegance.

THIS PRIVATE RETREAT (once a garden shed) has been outfitted with siding and roofing that match the owner's home.

If You Build It...

THE OWNER OF THIS NORTH CAROLINA PROPERTY wanted to transform an old shed into a personal and cozy home office. Sadly, the aged structure didn't survive the move to a new location in the yard, so she turned to plan B, asking the builder who was renovating the main house to construct a new 250-foot model. The result, as seen on these pages, is a quiet place for the owner to design and paint, as well as an idyllic locale for backyard barbecues.

▲ **TO MAKE THE MOST OF THE PAVILION'S CLOSE PROXIMITY TO THE GARDEN,** the owner placed an antique table next to the side door and set it up as an improved potting shed.

◄ **INSIDE THE COTTAGE, A VINTAGE BAMBOO SOFA AND CHAIR SET,** discovered at a flea market, was revived with new cushions covered in Sunbrella fabric.

A Greenhouse Goes Glam

THE HUSBAND OF THE OWNER OF THIS PROPERTY outside Vancouver took apart a neglected potting shed and rebuilt it into a greenhouse with a tempered-glass room. He added large windows found at a salvage yard to take in views of the peach trees, flowers, and vegetable gardens. The inside is furnished with vintage-floral pillows, white-painted furniture, and collections of mint-green Jadeite and milk glass vases. It's an escape just right for curling up with a book or chatting with company.

▼ THIS 10-BY-12-FOOT GREENHOUSE-inspired retreat started out as a shed. Now it's all gussied up and shaded by peach trees and Concord grapevines. Raised beds of carrots, corn, beets, and dill line the path to the door.

INSIDE, LUSH, FEMININE FLORALS
and remade castoffs lend a homey feel
to the one-room hideaway.

THE CRYSTAL CHANDELIERS
are just for show—no wiring—but
what a dazzling effect!

AN OLD LADDER becomes an inspired display for cups and vases filled with blooms from the garden just outside.

Clearly Ingenious

ADMITTEDLY, NOT EVERYONE has the talent to design and create a standout structure like this one, but there are plenty of brilliant ideas here that anyone can borrow. Note the bifold doors made from old windows and the iron gate flanked by roses ('Golden Celebration,' *right*, and 'Glamis Castle,' *left*) that frame the view.

▼ THE OWNER OF THIS KENTUCKY PROPERTY painstakingly attached glass doors and windows he'd collected for years to fashion the striking glass house, where he and his partner hold dinner parties.

THE BIFOLD DOORS OF THE GLASS HOUSE
open onto a limestone path and cutting garden.
Vintage iron pendant lamps are customized with
wire lampshade frames.

Up a Tree

LUCKY GUESTS AT THIS PENNSYLVANIA SPREAD nest in the trees—literally! The rustic structure comes complete with windows to catch the breeze, and breakfast is served in bed.

▼ **AN ANTIQUE IRON BED** fits perfectly in this simple space.

◄ **THE HOMEOWNER BUILT THIS TREEHOUSE** with the help of a carpenter; he estimates it cost $5000 to construct from pine and raw cedar. A pulley-and-box system makes it easy to load in supplies, and an extension cord runs from the garage to power a small fan.

Ideas at Your Doorstep

VIRTUALLY ANY OUTBUILDING on your property presents an opportunity for creativity—in terms of use, plantings, and décor. And it always makes sense to be inspired by what's nearby. For example, the grass border at the Michigan pool house below mimics native grasses in the distance. And the former springhouse opposite is surrounded by shade-loving plantings dictated by the adjacent trees.

▼ **THE POOL HOUSE** at this Michigan vineyard provides a shaded deck, with awning curtains for extra protection from the elements. A stand of inexpensive ornamental grass looks great year-round and affords privacy without blocking views.

A WITTILY MOUNTED
STAGHORN FERN welcomes
visitors to an old springhouse
now used as a guest cottage.

twine

6 AND

1

catalogs

2

5

picnic

4

8

pots

3

A carport becomes a garden shed and clever storage.

(1) A convenient iron dispenser keeps twine from getting tangled and hangs from any hook.

(2) A secondhand card catalog doubles as a brilliant filing system for seed packets. Any recipe box will fit the bill too.

(3) Pull a bait and switch on the tackle box. The fisherman's friend proves ideal for all those little odds and ends—twist ties, nails, etc.—that tend to get lost.

(4) The fix for wayward flowerpot saucers—a vintage dish drainer. This basic sink accessory, which rarely costs more than a couple of bucks at flea markets, organizes a bunch of basins in neat order.

(5) These jute-lined bins mean you can toss a mix of stuff inside and still maintain a lovely united front.

(6) Soda-pop crates provide the perfect nook for pillar candles. The slots of a nostalgic beverage box are just right for hard-to-stash lights.

(7) A carpenter's caddy finds a new calling. Tuck plant markers, stakes, and other small tools in one of these handled (read: easy-to-tote-outside) cases.

(8) Pop a cork in a beverage or condiment bottle and voilà—you have a spot for seeds or bird feed.

113

| 7 |

DECORATING WITH
CONTAINERS, VINES & MORE

PLANTS ARE LIKE A PAINTER'S PALETTE for the landscaper, creating beauty on the porch and beyond. And while perennial borders and cutting gardens certainly have their place, if you're looking for maximum impact with minimum effort (and let's be honest, who isn't?), containers, fast-growing vines, and a few other shortcuts are your new best friends.

Formal Dress

THE DESIGNERS OF BOTH OF THESE IMPRESSIVE GARDENS recruited humble pots to add grace notes—in one case, flowers, in another, boxwoods—proving that containers have a welcome place in any landscape.

➤ **POTS OF BOXWOODS** complement the loose, informal mix of nicotiana, sweet alyssum, and dahlias in the two beds flanking the stone path.

▲ **PLANTS IN SIMPLE POTS PUNCTUATE THE PATHWAY** of this formal boxwood-enclosed garden in Ohio. The century-old stone lion and brick pavers only enhance the appeal.

The Center of Attention

HANDSOME URNS make a beautiful statement and they beg to be admired. They can share the space with perennials in a border, or hold the floor solo as in the gravel courtyard below. Fill them with flowers, vines, or grasses—or a mixture of all three—and enjoy a graceful addition to the garden.

▼ **FRAMED BY WISTERIA,** a Grecian-style planter holds a tangle of geraniums and sweet-potato vines. Note that the iron fence also serves as a trellis!

◄ **IRON URNS FILLED WITH SPIKY GRASSES AND TRAILING FLOWERS** provide elegant accents throughout this Connecticut property. This one is a focal point in the poolside border.

Big or Small?

POTS CAN HAVE AN IMPACT any number of ways. A large container filled with a single striking specimen—such as a ficus tree, at right—can be a standout (all the more when matched with a partner). Or, mass smaller pots together and fill them with mounding plants, below. The climbing vines behind give the space a cozy, been-there-forever feeling.

➤ AN ARCHED STONE DOORWAY framed by ficus trees grandly leads the way to this home's main entrance.

▼ A VARIETY OF POTTED PLANTS PROVIDE A "BED" for the clematis and confederate jasmine that climb the brick wall that adjoins this back patio in Alabama.

THIS 1937 BIRMINGHAM, ALABAMA, TUDOR-STYLE COTTAGE is covered in a mix of 'Veilchenblau' and 'New Dawn' climbing roses.

Going Up

IT'S ENTIRELY POSSIBLE there is nothing more charming than climbing roses clambering over a doorway. To avoid visual confusion, stick to one or two complementary varieties—and then stand back and watch the show, year after year after year.

▼ **A LAVISH LOOK** is achieved with just two varieties of climbing rose: 'William Baffin' and 'New Dawn.' The key to creating this kind of drama? Planting a few types, but doing it in big sweeps.

Lush Life

BRING IT ON! The abundant vines here feature small white blossoms in season but the real payoff is their just-doesn't-quit foliage. Use them to cover an eyesore, or draw attention to a favorite feature.

➤ **WISTERIA VINES** set off the beautiful reclaimed windows of this sugar shack now used as a guest house. Below, oak leaf hydrangeas and lady's mantle bloom.

▲ **SWEET AUTUMN CLEMATIS** doesn't just grow tall (up to 30 feet in a few months)—it also grows wide, ensuring full coverage. Consider its tiny white flowers, which bloom in late summer and early fall, a bonus. Even more good news: It tolerates most soil and sun conditions.

THE BACK OF THIS 1915 RHODE ISLAND COTTAGE is covered in English ivy and shaded by oaks.

Green Scene

WHEN VINE MEETS HOUSE, the results can be high-octane. The English ivy on the roof at left gives the place the feel of an enchanted fairy-tale cottage. Morning-glory vines framing the porch below provide flowers during the daytime and a sweet, heart-shaped leaf "curtain."

▼ **A MORNING-GLORY AWNING** shades the porch by day, without blocking light from sun-loving agapanthus and pineapple lily below. West Indian teak chairs flank the cast-iron table, illuminated in the evening by a vintage hanging oil lamp.

Little Touches

EVEN MODEST PLANTS IN ORDINARY TERRA-COTTA POTS can add beauty, whether nestled against an out-building (below) or supplying ambience on a porch (right).

➤ **POTS OF MARGUERITE DAISIES, LAVENDER, AND ALLIUMS** brighten the porch off the library of this upstate New York home.

▲ **HUMBLE POTS** paired with statuary on a bench hover above a mint garden, creating a small, special moment.

Simple Perfection

OVERTHINKING ISN'T NECESSARY when it comes to unearthing the perfect containers for outdoor spaces. It's all good, from pretty stone-covered planters like the one on the opposite page to an ordinary kitchen colander (near right).

▲ **AN ENAMELWARE COLANDER** is repurposed as an outdoor planter with perfect drainage.

▶ **A STONE-COVERED PLANTER** is the footnote that takes this beachside outdoor shower from lovely to utterly idyllic.

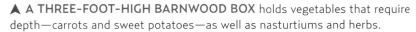

▲ **A THREE-FOOT-HIGH BARNWOOD BOX** holds vegetables that require depth—carrots and sweet potatoes—as well as nasturtiums and herbs.

▶ **A POTTED BEGONIA** in a humble straw basket adorns an outdoor table.

Surprise, Surprise!

A DEPARTURE FROM THE USUAL GARDEN FEATURES can delight, and help you see nature in a new way. An old sink (below) is a lovely counterpoint to vibrant fresh vegetables. Not one birdhouse—but a row of them—is eye-catching and impactful (opposite).

▼ **AN OLD SINK,** set atop a found-wood pedestal, offers a convenient spot for hosing off vegetables in a Martha's Vineyard garden.

◄ **THIS GARDEN IS DEFINED** by a combination of horticulture and structure. The line of bluebird houses provides the suggestion of a garden wall.

The Sky's the Limit

FOR THOSE WHO ARE SHORT ON SPACE, window boxes and vertical gardens offer an opportunity for planting. But even if you've got plenty of acreage, going up in addition to out has beautiful rewards.

▲ IF YOU HAVE A FENCE OR WALL YOU WANT TO BEAUTIFY, consider a vertical garden. Pockets—made of a breathable, recycled material akin to felt, sold individually or in rows of three or five—can last twenty years. Metal grommets make them easy to attach to a wall with screws.

THINK OUTSIDE THE (WINDOW) BOX

WHAT CAN YOU DO WITH A PLAIN WOODEN PLANTER? Just take a look at the four ideas here! Be sure to use a medium-weight potting mix that includes perlite and vermiculite—minerals that help keep soil aerated and prevent water loss. And fertilize once a week with a water-soluble formula diluted to one-quarter the recommended strength.

THE STARTING POINT: a plain white box.

THIS PLAIN PLANTER WAS DECORATED WITH "LACE." After sketching a leaf-inspired pattern on the box (which was already painted with white latex), the designer drilled holes and stitched them up with waxed cotton cord. Inside: strawberry plants, chives, and basils, along with columbines and trailing Sutera.

BIRCHBARK attached with epoxy to a plain window box provides a rustic front. Inside: chartreuse, yellow-flowered Bidens ferulifolia, and salvia.

DESIGNED TO MIMIC A SOUTHWESTERN LANDSCAPE, this stand-alone window box is set off by a sheet of brilliant blue acrylic screwed into its back. The box was sanded and stained with gray paint. Inside: Spiky Haworthia attenuata and two different sedums. The succulents are surrounded by tiny pebbles to keep excess moisture from reaching their stems.

THE SIDES OF THIS PLAIN WINDOW BOX are covered in a mosaic made from the shards of vintage teacups and trimmed in yellow-painted crown molding. Inside: plants that can be used to make herbal tea—chocolate spearmint, 'Kentucky Colonel' mint, German chamomile, pineapple sage, French lavender, and lemon-scented geraniums.

| 8 |

OUTDOOR
ENTERTAINING

FROM PICNICS TO COZY DINNERS FOR FOUR to big bashes meant for a crowd, welcoming guests to your home is always more fun when the party's outside. What follows: ideas to create special entertaining areas and inspirations for setting an extraordinary table. It's time for fun!

OPPOSITE At dinnertime, an antique trestle table glows with light from the home-owner's collection of gas lamps and lanterns.

Rustic Revelry

A RUNDOWN CABIN AND A SIMPLE TABLE ALL POSSESS ENTER-
TAINING POTENTIAL. While some people might see an old outbuilding
as nothing more than a storage shed, this homeowner envisioned it as a
centerpiece for festive gatherings. No outbuildings? Drag a table outside
and invite your friends!

▼ **THE OWNER OF THIS OHIO RETREAT**
turned a cabin into an enchanting party space
flanked by more than eighty 'Annabelle'
hydrangea bushes.

TWO HUMBLE (AND MISMATCHED) BENCHES plus a wooden table are all you need to turn an outdoor space into a party "room." Add a tablecloth topped with bounty and let the fun begin. No shoes required!

Good Times, Homemade

PUT YOUR OWN PERSONAL SPIN ON A PARTY with homemade décor and treats. There's no need for takeout pizza when the patio boasts a wood-burning pizza oven. And a gay DIY garland of linen handkerchiefs strung up with colorful ribbon on a white rope makes everyday outdoor furniture special.

▼ MOST COOKING AT THIS LITCHFIELD, CONNECTICUT, HOME TAKES PLACE OUTDOORS, thanks to an Italian wood–burning pizza oven (seen here), a stone grill, a fire pit, and a brick built–in barbecue with a rotisserie.

◄ DON'T FORGET THE DETAILS: Once you've made the simple (but delightful) garland, get ready for company with a comfy pillow, a bottle of chilled rose, and a quartet of welcoming glasses.

Set the Stage

OUTDOOR ENTERTAINING SPACES BENEFIT FROM INDOOR DÉCOR TECHNIQUES. A backdrop of gorgeous greenery is wonderful, but dressed up with assorted still life paintings, it's even better. Accessories like a hanging birdhouse, colorful pillows, and mismatched chairs in unexpected fabrics go way beyond the usual picnic table and gingham cloth. Talk about a fresh idea!

➤ **A WALL OF CLIMBING FIG SETS THE STAGE** for a collection of paintings (even those created by kids look wonderful in groups) which in turn create an intimate area within a larger party space.

▲ **A POLISHED-UP PLANK-STYLE PICNIC TABLE** is flanked by curved-back armchairs and a Lutyens bench. The pillows are splashed with bright pink.

A BAMBOO FOLDING TABLE AND BENCH set up shop beside a gorgeous field of grasses. Civilizing influences? A coordinating rug, pillow, and tablecloth, and yellow flower centerpieces.

Dinner on the Grounds

IN SUMMERTIME, WHEN THE LIVING IS FAMOUSLY EASY, meals almost beg to be served outside. A folding table like the bamboo number to the left travels easily for a casual meal. For a more formal affair, crisp white plates and lots of glassware dress things up while bright pink napkins, a table runner, and a flash of wood say, "dressy, but not *too* dressy."

▼ MAKE IT A GARDEN PARTY with repeating arrangements of single philo-dendron leaves partnered with clusters of delicate 'Limelight' hydrangeas in simple glass containers. Sprigs of fresh mint in the glasses contribute to the theme.

Romantic Woodland Supper

CONJURE UP A LUSH SCENE that feels fairy-tale enchanted—yet not too formal—with glowing candlelight, untamed greenery, and a flora-and-fauna motif.

▲ **INVITING IDEAS:** Little touches like ribbon and a tube mailer add up to a truly special delivery.

◄ **FERN FRONDS ARE NATURAL PLACEMATS,** and menu cards adorned with winged creatures help the fanciful theme take flight.

► **THIS TABLE MIXES COMMON HOUSEHOLD ITEMS AND WORTH-IT SPLURGES.** The centerpiece is primarily forsythia snipped from the garden, and the tablecloth is a matelassé bedspread. Instead of pricey store-bought lanterns, repurposed glass kitchen jars serve as candleholders.

French Country Fête

TIMELESS STRIPED LINENS, rattan accents, and citrusy colors evoke a midday meal in the Provence countryside.

▲ **A RATTAN-RIMMED INVITATION** promises a relaxed but sophisticated night. The expected envelope is pushed aside by a box mailer.

◄ **WILDLY PATTERNED SALAD DISHES** are paired with witty ceramic takes on the plain white paper plate. The favor: A pyramid-shaped gift box filled with bonbons.

► **A BASKET PILED HIGH WITH FRUIT** works as both an easy-to-achieve focal point and a refreshing dessert. Turned width-wise, traditional Basque runners create a casual play on placemats. Lamp-shaped votive holders bring interior panache outside, and terra-cotta pots supply an earthy place for pillar candles.

Sunset Fish Fry

WITH BLUES AND GREENS REMINISCENT OF A RAMBLING RIVER
plus ready-for-camp accessories (metal plates, classic lanterns), this tablescape is sure to reel guests right in.

▲ **GUESTS WILL ANGLE TO RSVP** when they receive this balsa-wood card nestled in a fly-fishing tin.

➤ **A PAINTED TROUT-SHAPED BOX** filled with a handful of Swedish fish candy is a cheeky treat.

◀ **BRIMMING WITH DILL AND QUEEN ANNE'S LACE,** an old fishing creel finds new use as a planter, and a vintage store display is reborn as a menu holder. Underneath, a camp blanket doubles as an unexpectedly lovely summertime tablecloth.

The Genteel Way to Go Wild

CALLING ALL AMATEUR BOTANISTS AND EXPLORERS!
Bring an air of refinement to your next garden party by celebrating
Victorian fascinations.

▲ **A FRESH ALTERNATIVE TO FLOWERS,** galvanized tin pedestals elevate sheet moss and mushrooms to centerpiece status.

◄ **SIMPLY SANDWICH A FERN FROND** between two inexpensive glass plates for an all-natural china pattern. Basswood chargers can be used again and again.

► **WOODLAND-INSPIRED DELIGHTS—** rustic sliced-log chargers, mushroom-and-moss centerpieces, and ferns and herbs—grace this festive table.

An ingenious home-owner created an inviting outdoor entertaining space—on a budget!

1. The basic workaday 12-by-8-foot storage shed kit was purchased from a big-box store. Cost? $958.

2. The shed's pre-hung opaque doors were swapped out for a glass-fronted French pair to let in more light.

3. By nailing a sheet of decorative heather fencing (less than $100) to each side of the roof, the owner cleverly mimicked the look of thatching.

4. Urn finials give the roofline flourish.

5. Raised beds filled with flowers and vegetables line the path to the doors. The sides of the utilitarian rot-resistant cedar frames are faced with ornamental willow fencing—the outdoor equivalent of icing a cake.

6. The walls and tables inside the shed are draped with linen fabric. On the exterior, two architectural mirrors create a trompe l'oeil effect.

PHOTOGRAPHY CREDITS

COVER

Front—Laura Moss

Back—(top) Gridley + Graves, (lower left) Ellen McDermott, (lower right) Keith Scott Morton

Melanie Acevedo: 80

Lucas Allen: 4 (bottom row right), 9, 10, 20, 40, 54, 60, 90, 107, 108, 109, 154

Quentin Bacon: 145

Christopher Baker: 26, 32 (right), 58, 69, 82, 106, 107, 119, 126, 130 (bottom right), 133

Andre Baranowski: 94

Justin Bernhaut: 63, 96

Stacey Brandford: 4 (middle row left), 53, 55, 57

Jane Booth Vollers: 118

Charlie Colmer & Jan Baldwin: 84

Roger Davies: 21, 56, 146, 147—151

Miki Duisterhof: 38, 50—52, 141

Jessica Hibbard Elenstar: 134

Don Freeman: 117

Dana Gallagher: 28

Getty images: Silvia Jansen, 7, 23, 25, 39, 41, 59, 77, 79, 93, 115, 137, 155

Tria Giovan: 145

Gridley + Graves: 47, 74, 75, 131

Gross & Daley: 17

Alison Gootee: 45, 130 (top right)

Audrey Hall: 8 (left)

Aimee Herring: 30

Alec Hemer: 4 (top row left, middle row right), 19 (right), 33, 35, 61, 64, 72, 87, 114

Lisa Hubbard: 4 (bottom row right), 78, 88, 123, 132

Lynn Karlin: 124

Max Kim-Bee: 4 (middle row center), 12, 15, 24, 37, 65, 68, 89, 91, 99, 111, 125, 128, 129, 160

Mark Lohman: 14 (top right)

James Merrell: 8 (right), 32 (left), 138, 139

Karyn Millet: 135, 143

Laura Moss: 6, 19 (left), 44, 62, 97, 120, 122

Janis Nicolay: 102—105

Marcus Nilsson: 81

Michael Partineo: 136

Victoria Pearson: 4 (top row right), 11, 14 (bottom right), 22, 43, 46, 48, 67, 70, 71, 86, 130 (left), 152, 153

Steven Randazzo: 13 (right), 116, 127

Lisa Romerein: 36, 66

Tina Rupp: 144

Lisa Sacco: 83

Keith Scott Morton: 16, 49, 100, 101, 142

William P. Steele: 92, 121

Tim Street-Porter: 14 (left)

Robin Stubbert: 95

STUDIO D: Alison Grootee, 140

Jonny Valiant: 18, 27

Bjorn Wallander: 31, 42, 76

William Waldron: 13 (left), 29, 73

Richard Warren: 34, 110

INDEX